PART OF LIFE'S RICH TAPESTRY

PART OF LIFE'S RICH TAPESTRY

BY

BARBARA HASLER

December 1996

© Copyright - Barbara Hasler

Published by:
Barbara Hasler

Printed by:
ProPrint
Riverside Cottage
Great North Road
Stibbington
Peterborough
PE8 6LR

ISBN: 0 9529659 0 9

CONTENTS

No Fixed Abode	1
An Artist's Story	2
Barbara	3
Jesus Is Coming To Dine	4
Bay Of Tranquillity	5
Christmas 1994	6
Bosnia '95	8
A Boy's Story	9
The Carpenter	10
The Invitation	12
The Angel	14
Civil War	15
Come	16
Daddy Mend It	18
The Baby	19
Worship	20
The Disciple	22
The Druggie	23
What Do You See?	24
Easter	26
The Road To Emmaus	27
To Be Sung To The Tune Eventide (Abide With Me)	28
The Oriana Inaugural Season - Before The Cruise	29
The Oriana Inaugural Season - After The Cruise	30
Christmas	32
Gifts	34
God	35
What Is God Like	36
The Greenhouse Theory	38
Harvest	39
Insomnia	40
Kobe	41
A Lament	42
London	43
And Evening Street - London	44
A Magical Feeling	45

Winning The Lottery	46
Missing The Mark	48
Mary - Mother To Be	49
Mary Joan	50
Jarius' Daughter	52
Memories	54
Moses	55
News	56
Passover	58
The Pool Of Bethesda	60
Our Railway	62
The Seagull	63
The Seat 1994	64
Early Spring - Scilly	65
Summer '95	66
English Summer	67
Summer Night	68
New Teeth	69
Temptation	70
The Miracle	72
The Tourist Trade	74
Hotel Breakfast	75
A Mother	76
The Lord's Prayer	77

NO FIXED ABODE

I haven't washed my hair for months.
My head is covered with lice.
I look for food in the rubbish bins,
Which I share with the rats and mice.
My bedding I keep in a plastic bag.
There's nothing like papers for heat,
For I lie in a cardboard box at night,
With plimsolls on my feet.
My friends are drunk, or drugged, or mad.
They fear neither wet nor gloom.
They do not see the notice large,
That says, 'This way the tomb'.
And many times I have been given
A lodging for day and for night.
But staying inside, away from the air,
Just doesn't feel that right.
And why not end it all, my friend,
They say - 'Life must be like hell'.
But then, they do not understand,
There's advantages as well.
I'm not tied down to time or place.
I can wander wherever I will.
So it looks like I shall stay as I am.
And you say to me - 'Until?'

AN ARTIST'S STORY

The little child had been extremely ill,
And months before had hovered by death's door,
Malnourished; father a drunken sot,
Ill-used she typified the hungry poor.

She then, when well enough to leave her bed,
From hospital to convalesce was sent.
Grim walls, tenderness all unknown,
Regulations abounded; none were bent.

Nobody called to see just how she was,
And then, one Sunday, early in the day,
'A treat,' they said, and dressed her in her best.
'Come,' they said to her, 'This is the way.'

They took her out to sit among the flowers
Out in a garden she had never seen.
'Stay there,' they said, 'surprise will come your way.'
She sat to wait. Whatever did they mean?

Sitting so quiet, eyes shut in the sun,
She heard the song of birds, the hum of bees,
And looking, saw the wonder of God's world,
The colours of the garden, sky and trees.

All day she sat drinking the vision in,
God's healing power wiping away the past,
Till grinding hunger and the fear of dark,
Drove her to tap upon the door at last.

Busy within, by all she'd been forgotten,
Who hours before had sat her in the air,
To wait a visit from a loveless mother,
Who hadn't called; who really didn't care.

But she who didn't know for whom she waited
Had from a loving Father gifts been given
The gift to paint the beauties that He'd shown her,
A little stay with Him in that sweet Heaven.

BARBARA

She's called Barbara, caquehanded and fool.
Like her name, she's a stranger in life.
For she follows the beat of a drummer called Love,
That involves her in sorrow and strife.
This Love understands her desires.
This Love reads her mind as his own.
He holds her, supports her, leads her on when she tires.
To bring her at last to his throne.
If you seek for this drummer called Love
You may find the way narrow and long,
But the joy as you go, knowing how you are loved
Is the reason for singing this song.

JESUS IS COMING TO DINE

'Jesus is coming to dine tonight,' she said, as she cleaned the fish,
Then she piled the peaches and plums and grapes into a lordly dish.
'He's walked the roads with His friends for weeks. They'll be dirty
                                      and sticky and hot.
But perhaps we will hear how the Kingdom comes, and the followers
                                      they have got.'

'Jesus is coming to dine tonight,' said he as he slid down the tree.
'Jesus is coming to eat in my house - Jesus - He's chosen me!
Now wife, you must give Him the best you can. You have no idea
                                      of the joy
That He's given me here in my heart today, that I'll pass on to
                                      all I employ!'

'Jesus is coming to dine tonight,' said they, 'For the Passover's here,
But we fear for His safety. We fear for His life, and we feel there
                                      is suffering near.
We hope He is bringing His own Kingdom in, but He seems to be
                                      fighting a war,
Which shows in His face, full of beauty and grace, of sorrow and
                                      sadness in store.'

Jesus is coming to dine tonight, though we don't know it now on
                                      the road,
Where we've walked and we've talked till the evening has come and
                                      we've shared with Him all of the load
Of our sorrow that He who was hung on a tree we had seen as our
                                      Master and King.
But His hands will proclaim of His rising again and our prayers and
                                      His praises we'll sing.

Is Jesus coming to dine tonight with you and with me and with us?
Is the door open to welcome Him in with no more excuses and fuss?
While wishing to give Him the best that we are, surprisingly so we
                                                                          shall find
That He will feed us with His Body and Blood - offered for all
                                                                          humankind.

BAY OF TRANQUILLITY

Into the clear, pellucid depths I peered,
To watch the fronded weed wave to and fro.
Pale jade above the sanded floor
The water flowed beneath my questing toe.

Cerulean blue reflecting bluer sky,
Where depths of time and distance fade away,
And gulls dip in the tranquil air
Across the water of the sunny bay.

Small sparkling jewels of beaded water smile,
To edge the rocks with borders pure and white,
Glistening with mermaids tears,
Like bridal ribbons in the morning light.

O that I could always stay like this,
A dreamland far from all that brings us down,
But often clouds disguise the scene
And back I go to bustle and to town.

Small drops of beauty lie within our lives.
We treasure signs of love that spring anew.
Remember that God knows our needs,
And trust Him always, though these drops are few.

CHRISTMAS 1994

Have you finished writing Christmas Cards?
Have you iced the Christmas cake?
Have you found the decorations?
Mum, are you quite awake?

Have you done the pies for Saturday?
Have you ironed my fancy dress?
Have you sorted out the presents?
You have? Well, more or less.

Is there something for the milkman?
And the postie, and the dust?
Don't forget to get some bread in.
You have ordered cream, I trust?

Sue has gone all vegetarian,
So she won't touch the bird.
Don't forget some veggie burgers.
Over Christmas? That's absurd.

Don't forget to have your hair set.
Don't forget the shops will shut.
Will you leave off nagging at me?
The fairy lights have just gone phut!

Is there any food today? Mum
Will you stand behind that queue?
What is it they are selling?
Any sort of food will do.

Is it rather tired cabbage?
Can you boil it up for soup?
With a turnip or potato
Will it fill? How big a group?

Is it dusty, weevily flour?
Can we really make some bread?
Can you hear the women crying
For another loved one dead?

Can you spare a little water
So that I can wash my hair?
It's so greasy Mum, and gritty.
Have you any soap to spare?

Can we light a little candle,
Upon this Christmas morn,
To celebrate the birthday
When the Prince of Peace was born?

BOSNIA '95

Displaced, bereaved, we set out weeping on an unknown way,
And in the burning sun we curse the day,
And walk.

Behind, now lost, our homes, our fields, our livelihoods, our crops.
Ahead the road, no food, no drink, no stops.
Death follows.

Time was when our side sent the enemy out to leave the fruitful land.
Expelled them cruelly with a violent hand,
Or killed.

We did not think that we should need the houses that they burnt.
The lesson hatred teaches still unlearnt.
Hope dies.

Only when suffering hits us fair between our disbelieving eyes
Do some of us remember all the lies,
Absorbed.

Others learn nothing, only weep for vengeance to the brazen skies,
Asking no questions of the hows or whys,
But blood.

A BOY'S STORY

I wish to be a pilot and fly across the sky.
I want to be in charge of things, or know the reason why.
I think I'll drive a chopper and hover over rocks
And rescue people from the cliffs without their shoes and socks.

So I went to the heliport to see how choppers work,
If I was to be a pilot then my training I'd not shirk.
Men in overalls were testing every bit of that big chopper.
It is vital that it's tested, so it doesn't come a cropper.

'The pilot may not fly,' they said, 'until we've passed it sound.
If we miss a fault that's growing, it may hurtle to the ground.
So we're far more important than the pilot, don't you see?
How much more important than the ground staff are you wanting
                                                                            now to be?'

They took me round the chopper and they showed me all the dials.
Electric circuits, switches, wires, there were miles and miles
                                                                             and miles.
They showed me the big rotor blades and there right at the top
Was a nut that's really vital, if the blades are not to stop.

Since it keeps the lot together, and it keeps it all in place.
And it keeps it running sweetly, else it's sudden death you face.
So I thought about that visit. Chopper pilots there are few.
And they rely on lots of men, not only just the crew.

So whether I think I'm in charge, or know I'm very lowly,
We have to find our place in life, and learning that comes slowly.
The nut atop a chopper is called the Jesus nut,
And like it, without His presence our happiness goes phut!

THE CARPENTER

He had been a chippie for twenty years.
His work had been with wood.
He had sawn it, planed it, nailed it through.
He had shaped it where He could.
He had taken over His father's job,
For Joseph had died by then,
And He toiled long hours for good results,
Much better than other men.
His mother would stand and watch His skill,
As He shaped a yoke or table,
And think of the years that had passed by
Since His birth in that distant stable.

And now He stood on the mountain top
In a robe of glistening white,
Whilst beside Him stood those two of old,
On left hand and on right.
I could not look into His face,
For the light was too much to bear,
And I fell before Him in wonder and awe,
For His beauty was bright and fair.
And a voice like the roar of the ocean shore,
Filled the air of that lonely hill;
'This is my Son, my Beloved One,
Who is pleased to do My will.'

So we glimpsed for a moment a man made God,
Transfigured with light and power.
We saw Him then as a King of Kings,
Our castle, our rock, our tower.
We saw Him as He ever shall be,
Beyond this time and space,
And He shall over everyone reign,
No matter their colour or race.
But He was a chippie and worked with wood.
He lived with us for a span.
And He died on a cross that we made for Him;
For our beautiful God, made man.

THE INVITATION

'Come,' I said, 'And walk with me,
Come and be my guide,
Come and help me with this life.
Come and let me hide
There beneath Your shadow great,
There beneath Your wing.
Come and tell me what to do.
Come and make me sing.'

But in the ensuing quiet,
Nothing could I hear.
No one seemed to hear my plea.
There seemed no one near.
And I walked a lonely road.
Alone beside me kept
Pace with all my faltering steps
Fear, and doubting crept.

These my close companions now.
Where had I gone wrong?
Where the Lord who loves me so?
He could make me strong.
Like a light upon the way
Suddenly I knew
What is was that I had missed,
What |I had to do.

Jesus said, 'Come follow Me,'
I must follow Him.
Not that He would follow me
Along my path of sin.
'Take my will and let me be
One with You,' I said.
I will follow where *You* lead.
You will be my Head.

'Not my will, but Yours,' I cry,
Though my heart rebel.
Though I often drift away,
And Your words repel.
'Keep me in Your hand,' I plead,
'Fashion me anew.'
And the answer loud came back,
'This is what I'll do.

Give me everything you hold,
Everything you own;
Fears and hopes and all desires.
Place them at My throne.
Careless you must now become;
Carefree as a bird,
Knowing that I'll hold them all,
Knowing that I've heard.

THE ANGEL

The sweetest odour filled the air;
A soft-as-feather sound.
I lifted up my weary eyes,
From looking on the ground.

For there beside me I had sensed
A being bright and fair,
With golden sandals on his feet,
And gold band round his hair.

From royal purple near the ground,
To white behind his head,
His wings swept round with colours bright
Of yellow, blue and red.

He didn't speak, he only stood,
And held me with his arm,
And looked at me with loving eyes,
That caused me no alarm.

The years have passed and I've not seen
This heavenly being again,
But well I know he walks with me,
Through sorrow and through pain.

Be sure, when life is good or bad,
You cannot be mistaken.
Your guardian angel's by your side,
Until to God you're taken.

CIVIL WAR

What are you thinking as you sit there
Alone on that seat in the square so bare?
What awful sights hang before your eyes,
That see, unseeing what round you lies?
Were you always alone in an upstairs flat?
Are you used to no one living near?
Have you just lost another - a sister, a brother,
A husband, a child that is dear?
Is your home laid flat? Can't you handle that?
Does the plastic sheet hold your possessions?
Are you hoping to find in the depths of your mind
Understanding of all these transgressions?
And there near your feet is a misfired shell.
Were you sitting there when beside you it fell?
My words have no meaning that I can tell
For your mind had switched off from this awful hell.
And the snow and the cold numbs your weary brain
As you sit watching slayer and slain,
You may die of a bullet that's not meant for you,
Or drift off in sleep as the cold eats through.
For those who live far from this battlefield,
You're a symbol of Spirit that will not yield,
A symbol of waste of the blessings of life
By the devil of power and the devil of strife.

COME

Who me? You must be joking.
You can't be calling me.
I've ridiculed and scorned You.
I would not bow the knee.

I've joined those who chorused,
'All Christians must be mad
To worship One who would not fight,
And died a death so bad.'

It's true, You could be cutting
To those whose pride was great.
You showed Your love to all the poor
And told us not to hate.

But how can I enjoy myself
And take my dates to bed,
And drink myself unconscious,
With You standing by my head.

How can I bash my girlfriend?
How can I pick a fight?
How can I pull a fast one,
With You standing in the light?

But You want me, You are saying.
You are nagging at my mind.
Follow You, You cannot mean it.
Can I leave all this behind?

True, I've never known another
Offer me such love and trust.
Can You deal with all my sinning,
With my lying and my lust?

Yes, You can, You say.
You're willing to take my life in hand,
Make it new, and so exciting.
Will You make me understand?

If You can fill the void
I seem to find inside,
Come on in, and make me different,
And all my friends beside.

DADDY MEND IT'

My Dad was clever,
He mended our toys.
'Daddy mend it,' we'd cry, and he did.
He had clever fingers, my mum used to say.
Patient endeavour.

He didn't say much,
As he beavered away,
With paper, and cardboard and glue.
The cleverest father of any, we said.
Lightest of touch.

I've seen others' toys,
In a big broken heap,
Or left all forlorn in a box.
Their dads weren't so clever, or just didn't care,
Ignore children's joys.

We all have a Dad,
Who is clever at mending.
Our broken lives He will make whole.
He cares when our lives are in pieces or rending.
Be joyful, not sad.

So come to His knee
And accept His great love
Without pride, and be grateful, my friend.
Just, 'Please, Daddy, mend it, whatever it takes.'
How happy He'll be.

THE BABY

Whose hands received You from the womb
Child of God?
What did Your weigh?
What colour were Your eyes, when Your took our clay?

Whose face did You first see there then
Child of God?
What did You hear?
What did You feel and see when she was near?

Whose rough hands touched Your still-wet head
Child of God?
Keepers of sheep
Came to see who was born when You were asleep.

Did they the angels round Your manger see
Child of God?
They saw them there
Where they had been sleeping on the cold hillside bare.

Can we come close to where You reign
Child of God?
May we adore
Not just this Holy night but for evermore?

WORSHIP

We won't have vain repetition,
Though we've had this prayer before,
And you'll find the words of the service
On the shelf behind the door.

We won't have vain repetition,
As we have said before,
But we've sung this chorus umpteen times
And we'll sing it now once more.

We won't have empty ritual.
We like what we have known,
For 'nothing changes here' we sing
And bow before Your throne.

We won't have empty ritual.
New actions we must bring,
But we'll swing our orgiastic hips
To everything we sing.

Of course it matters what you wear.
You come to meet your King.
You wear the best that you can find.
He'll notice everything.

The heart's the think that matters.
God's not looking at your gear.
Be comfortable to swing along,
For God is such a dear.

'Did I make my children boss-eyed,
So they keep their eyes on Me,
But can also carp and criticise
My loved ones that they see?'

If eyes are straight and to Me look,
Then I alone they'll measure.
The faults of them and of their friends
I'll tackle at *My* pleasure.

My love will fill their hearts with Joy.
They'll pass that Love along,
And all their differences erase
In singing of *My* song!

THE DISCIPLE

The crack and crunch of breaking bone,
A cry to pierce you through.
Then 'Father, now forgive them
For they know not what they do.'

A rock is hurled. Your servant reels,
And falls upon his knees.
'Don't put this sin upon their list.
Lord, hear Your servant's pleas.'

Another one stays by his friends
As one by one they die.
And prays for them and those who kill
Before with them he'll lie.

And one is knocked upon the head,
Beneath the ice is slid,
Because Your love meant more than death
And goodness can't be hid.

The fuse was set, the time had come,
And those who mourned the dead
Joined them in blood - a father wept.
'Father forgive,' He said.

'Father forgive,' we still must say
To follow in Your way.
That all the world may know His love,
And reach unending day.

THE DRUGGIE

Dirty, with dreadlocks and an earring,
He sat with a dog at his feet.
Loud rock'd left him quite hard of hearing.
Ah, the Walkman was pulsing a beat,
And he'd heard not the question I'd given,
As he lounged by the seat in the square.
'Did you know that your sins are forgiven,
Once you've said 'Yes' to Jesus? - You there,
Jesus loves you, in spite of your drugging,
Your rebellion, your swearing, and worse.
He died on a cross. 'Stop your tugging,'
He turned to his dog with a curse.
'Jesus loves me?' he said, 'I'm no homo.
I'm a man who needs bimbos to lay,'
For he didn't see how God could love us
In the midst of that dirt and decay.

But with eyes on the pavement he listened
When I tried to put God's love across,
Till he sniffed and his hollow cheeks glistened,
And he showed me his pain and his loss.
Then he followed me down for a Big Mac,
And a large tin of cola and chips.
He told me of his life as a druggie,
And the awful effects of the trips.
He told me he wanted to kick it,
If only someone cared enough
To be with him in hell when he got there,
To love when the going was tough.
So I put out one hand to my brother.
The other I gave to my Lord.
'Come, pull Lord, for here is another,
Who we'll save through the power of your sword.

WHAT DO YOU SEE?

When you close your eyes and pray,
Is Christ still a baby small?
Does He wave His tiny fists aloft,
Happy to be with us all?

When you close your eyes and pray,
What vision of Christ do you see?
Does He hang before you, pale and wan,
Dying for us on that terrible tree?

When you close your eyes and pray,
Does Christ kneel with you too?
In the desert of your searching soul
Does His presence carry you through?

When you close your eyes and pray,
Does the Risen Master greet you
In Heaven's triumphant loveliness?
Does He come to meet you?

When you close your eyes and pray,
Do you your King adore,
Who sits upon that heavenly throne,
And reigns in power for ever more?

When I close my eyes and pray,
My lovely King I own.
I bow adoring at His feet,
And worship Him upon the throne.

Scars of love shine from His hands,
Uplifted then to bless.
His robes shine with a radiance bright,
He all my greatest needs address.

And there He sits and reigns,
Till all His enemies confess,
That He alone is Lord and King,
And hastening to His side they press.

EASTER

The garden lay at peace beneath the setting moon,
That wove pale fingers through the olive trees.
The eastern sky was paling as the dawn comes soon,
And young leaves trembled in a fitful breeze.

Beside the tomb of rock three men were sitting, thinking;
Their lone night vigil coming to an end.
A useless occupation, sleep contending, eyelids blinking.
They lingered on where sleep and waking blend.

Another One was there. They woke into the gloom.
A crunch of gravel broke their fragile dreams,
And past them walked a man out from the tomb.
The moon displayed Him in its silver beams.

His shadow fell across the path - they stood transfixed,
Too terrified to stop His passage past.
He's gone, and feelings of relief and terror mixed,
The air was still, the rock tomb closed up fast.

But as they thought that no ill did betide,
A laugh turned them around. An angel dressed in white
Put out his hand and rolled the stone aside.
An empty tomb with graveclothes met their sight.

THE ROAD TO EMMAUS

No, no it can't be possible for dead is dead
And did you see that soldier pierce His side?
Yes, and I saw Him hanging when the life had sped.
No doubt at all the fact that He had died.

Then what about the women's story then?
But at that point I happened to turn round.
A man had joined us though I don't know when,
Was walking with us, three Emmaus bound.

A total stranger since he didn't know
The awful death our Master had just died.
He asked for details since we seemed so low,
And yet were somewhat mystified.

This man, this stranger started to explain
How Jesus had to die to save from sin
Rebellious humankind, and by His pain,
To o'ercome sin and our redemption win.

The night drew on. We to our lodging came.
'Stay,' we both cried. This traveller must not go.
He'd spoken to our hearts and lit a flame.
We did not question, 'Can this stranger know?'

How can He know what we have failed to see?
How can He know the yearnings of our soul?
Now we would fall before Him - bend the knee,
But then we knew not who would make us whole.

Only in breaking of the evening bread.
Only in blessing did we see the scars.
Then, only then, we saw - and He had sped,
Left us with joy, to run back 'neath the stars.

TO BE SUNG TO THE TUNE EVENTIDE (ABIDE WITH ME)

Once more the lottery's failed me - I've not won.
Hope for the next has not yet quite begun.
Trust that six million I will win, 'ere long,
Keeps up my spirits while I sing this song.

'Why do you want six million?' you will say.
'Only, my friend, to give it all away.'
Answering to churches' never-ending pleas,
'Give, give and give again. We're on our knees.'

'You should not gamble. Gambling is a sin.
With your beliefs you don't deserve to win.
Ends do not justify the means you take.
Pray for your wants, - 'Right, Lord, give us a break.'

THE ORIANA INAUGURAL SEASON
- BEFORE THE CRUISE

What shall I take when I go on my cruise?
What shall I take in my case?
I can take all my clothes but not possibly use,
And where can I find the space.

Where it is hot I shall need summer dresses,
Where it is cold, woolly sweaters.
A hat I might need to cover my tresses,
When I sit in the sun writing letters.

And everyone says, 'You will have a good time.
You will come back as fat as a pig,
For the lunches and dinners are truly sublime,
So you will not stay thin as a twig.'

We must run round the deck to keep weight in check,
And exercise madly together,
Unless we are saved from eating too much,
By some highly unfortunate weather.

When we'll lie on our beds looking greener than grass,
And wish we were totally dead,
Wishing and hoping the storm will soon pass,
And we can rise up from our bed.

We must not consider the worst that might come,
So jolly we'll be on our cruise.
So fill up your plate and fill up your tum,
And let us get blotto with booze.

Then we'll see all the places that warrant a visit,
And everyone will be so kind,
'You will love it, I tell you, it's super now' - is it?
I would sooner be staying behind.

THE ORIANA INAUGURAL SEASON - AFTER THE CRUISE

I'm back from my cruise, and everyone says,
'Now will you be going again?
Was it worth all the planning, the anticipation,
Did you lose all the stress and the strain?'

And I smile, and I nod, and I pull a wry face.
'It's a once in a lifetime event.
Now I can see how the other half lives.
I suppose that I'm glad that I went.'

When I say other half, I don't mean just the rich
For the social scene was so wide,
And the rich and the proud mixed with those who weren't bright.
Most returned, though not all, and one died.

They all wanted the best that could possibly be
For themselves. It was geared just for 'Me.'
'I, Me and Myself,' was the tone of the trip.
Little thought for their God, on the sea.

In Tangiers it was dirty, patriarchal and hot.
The men never stopped trying to sell
Anything that they had; till we really got angry,
And some told them, 'Off - go to Hell.'

Sidi Bel Said was clean and well kept,
But in Tunis they didn't like us.
They kept us all waiting with passports and forms,
Till the crew was fed up with the fuss.

Syracuse still was pleasant and warm,
And the people were friendly and kind.
We looked at some catacombs, ruins, papyrus,
And were sad to leave this place behind.

And on then to Naples, both stormy and wet,
Though Pompeii improved through the morning.
Forked lightning and thunder attended us later.
Gave the rest of the trip a sad warning.

For the wind it did blow and we passed Elba by,
Likewise Marseilles and Cadiz,
A few hours we had in lovely Lisbon,
But many began to feel miz.

Then a chopper took one of the passengers off.
He was too ill to finish the cruise.
And back late we steamed to our shores once again.
If you like, I can show you the views.

Oh, the food? It was good. It was brilliant in fact.
Everything one could wish for was found.
I'm allergic to milk products - that cuts out cream.
Now I'll weigh - I have lost half a pound!

CHRISTMAS

There are always people coming to our house.
They've been travelling the road for many a day.
They've sometimes come on camels from lands to the east,
And are tired after riding such a way.

And sometimes it's a soldier who rides up,
All dusty, with his horse looking beat.
'Fellow, get me a meal as quick as you can.
Fresh bread and new wine, and good meat.'

It was winter, and the weather it was cold.
And our house was full to bursting with these men.
I was standing at the door when another one came.
'No room,' Dad cried, 'We already have ten.'

This man was standing by the donkey's head,
On which there was a weary woman slumped.
And she was moaning quietly in the chill of the night,
I had to speak - how loud my heart then pumped.

'You've got to find a little space right now.
This lady's ill - she can't be sent away.
Oh Dad, if you can't give her a bed for the night,
Then what about the stable with the hay?

Dad shut me up, but then he turned around,
'You've got a point my little lass - that's it.
You are welcome to the stable where it's warm and dry.
Go, get a lamp, and I shall get it lit.'

I wriggled and I tossed on my mat.
The lady's face kept coming to my mind.
There was a hustle and a bustle around the house all night.
Then a baby's cry was heard on the wind.

There were jolly voices in the street outside,
And I recognised old Ben, the shepherd's laugh.
What on earth were they doing at that time of night?
Then the bleating of a lamb and a calf.

And I fell asleep wondering at the noise,
And the lady and her bed in the straw,
And woke to find a baby had been born in the night.
Then I hurried round to peep behind the door.

The lady was asleep by the man,
And everything was peaceful, quiet and still,
But over their heads I could see, as in a mist,
A man on a cross on a hill.

GIFTS

What do they want for Christmas?
What can I get this year?
It seems to get more and more difficult,
Christmas cheer.

What do they want for Christmas?
Money's so dull I think.
Aunty Rose wants some woolly gloves;
Bright pink.

What do they want for Christmas?
My mind is in a whirl.
T-shirts, books, or scent and discs;
Boy or girl?

What do we want for Christmas?
As into bed we climb.
Nothing that money can buy, but just
Your *time!*

GOD

God says:-

I do not live in temples built by hands,
Nor rest above the altars you have made.
You seek for Me mid rocks, and sea and sands,
But only see creation there displayed.

How can you put your maker in a box?
Or pin Me down? Who spreads the universe?
Think you can find Me in the aged rocks,
Who is, and ever will be? Which is worse?

Those who do not consider me at all,
And go about this life with clo-sed eye?
Or those who are quite sure they know it all,
Whose vision is so small, it's near a lie?

Love is my name. Confuse me not with lust.
My love will fill you with a sweetness new.
Dwells in your heart if you will only trust.
Alone I AM all that is good and true.

                                      Says God.

WHAT IS GOD LIKE?

Tell me, 'What is God like?'
I really wish I knew.
I just cannot imagine Him.
Can you?

Yes, God is like a father.
Our God is like your Dad.
He loves you and He works for you.
Be glad.

He's happy when we're joyful.
He's proud to see us grow.
He likes to see us take our place
You know.

We take to Him our troubles.
He'll help and give advice.
We know we can rely on Him.
That's nice.

Now you understand
What I've been trying to say;
God loves you as a father does.
Hooray!

His quiet reply was chilling,
'I never knew my Dad.
My Mum and boyfriends brought me up.
I'm sad.'

They said they would not marry.
They did not love enough
To give each other all they had!
That's tough.

How can I tell a father
Is loving, kind and true.
So tell me, 'What is God like?
Like you?'

THE GREENHOUSE THEORY

We must believe the experts,
We're having too much rain.
There's twice as much as normal.
It really is a bane.

We're told the land is sinking,
Under water, is it not?
It's the greenhouse theory linking
With the climate that we've got.

Ah, but now the sun is scorching
Everything that you can see.
We've not had any rain since March.
It's killing plant and tree.

And our land will be a desert.
There'll not be a hotter spot.
It's the greenhouse theory linking
With the climate that we've got.

I remember several years ago
We had a winter cold
And ice and snow up to the ears.
'It's the ice age,' we were told.

We are due for just another.
They would put it in this slot.
It's the greenhouse theory linking
With the climate that we've got!

HARVEST

Out of the sun-warmed air I came,
Turning the large ringed handle of the ancient door,
And stepped onto the cool and wide flagged floor,
And stood.

The air was sweet with scents well-known,
Bringing back memories of a distant past,
Harvest brought in, and gathering done at last.
Quiet peace.

Rosy-cheeked apples, polished to a shine,
Heaped high on sills, bedecked with autumn flowers,
Red-gold chrysanthemums and gladioli towers
Standing erect.

Sheaves of cut corn leaned pale against the pews,
And sun-kissed grapes hung from the pulpit's edge,
Tomatoes, plums, ripe fruit on every ledge,
Praising God.

Harvest, that time of work complete.
The labours of the year expressed in coloured scent.
The energies of God's creation spent -
The fruit.

And what of us? Our harvest when all's done?
What shall we pour before our Saviour Lord?
Will there be love and joy and sweetness and accord?
Our gifts?

INSOMNIA

O that I could but fall asleep,
And wearied limbs in sweet oblivion steep.
A few short minutes did I lose this world,
But back to consciousness was quickly hurled,
And sat straight up.

And from then on throughout the sticky night,
Whether I turned on left side or on right,
Or curled up tight or lay straight out,
With tumbled bedclothes falling all about,
Sleep fled my mind.

Quick as my thoughts unkempt, began to stray,
I pulled them back. They could not get away.
Tight were my muscles as a bowman's string.
Thoughts crowded in. I could not give them wing.
The hours crept by.

I rose, and ate and drank and tried to read,
And took some aspirin to help my need.
Yet, though I twitched, sleep now not far away,
I found it not, and now here comes the day
The seagulls cry.

O you who nightly go to bed and 'die',
Give thought to those, who, having shut the eye
Remain awake. Or only sleep with opiates that knock out,
But don't reduce the body's mental shout,
'Let me unwind'   Please.

KOBE

The earth shook, my life it took.
Where do I go from here?
Do all the slain live again?
Where do I go from here?
My Mum, my Dad
Are very sad
Where do I go from here?
I was not sick
And death was quick
Where do I go from here?
Say, being bright,
Answer me right,
Where do I go from here?

A LAMENT

She had fed him and washed him and changed his vest.
She had brought him up as she knew best,
And 'My baby, my baby, my baby,' she cried,
When she learnt that her soldier son had died.

She had watched him grow, and brushed his hair.
She had seen him toddle from chair to chair.
Then 'My baby, my baby, my baby,' she cried,
When she learnt that her soldier son had died.

She had welcomed in his school-day friends,
And coped with the ills that this world sends.
But 'My baby, my baby, my baby,' she cried,
When she learnt that her soldier son had died.

She rejoiced when he married his sweetheart true
And she married again, which would make life new.
Then 'My baby, my baby, my baby,' she cried,
When she learnt that her soldier son had died.

But he'd entered a life for the brave and bold.
That life was taken and my tale told.
'O my baby, my baby, my baby,' she cried,
When she learnt that her soldier son had died.

O God keep my baby, for he's now Your own,
Till we all meet again in front of Your throne.

LONDON

Hurrying feet,
Hustling noise.
Some things do not change
In thirty years since I walked the streets
Of the city where I was born.

Worried eyes,
Biting lips,
A city for the young.
There's too much stress for the wrinklies here
In the city where I was born.

Cleaner streets,
Fresher air,
Buildings bright and fresh.
Gone is the stench that I used to know
In the city where I was born.

Sudden death,
Blood and glass.
Some things do not change.
Memories of how it was, and is
In the city where I was born.

AN EVENING STREET - LONDON

'Man, it's cold. It's enough to freeze yer balls.
Have a copy of Big Issue will yer now?'
'Our tickets - are they circle, or are they in the stalls?'
'I shall take the 18:50 out to Slough.'

'Where can I stand where the wind won't blow?
Have a copy of Big Issue as you pass.'
'So I said to her, Stuff it! Let's go to a show.'
'Then blow me, but my hand went through the glass.'

'No one is buying these papers. Wot the hell.
Have a copy of Big Issue will you there?'
'What he meant when he said that I never could tell.'
'Keep it to yourself then. I don't care.'

'Don't you see us, you with homes, you with dosh.
Have a copy of Big Issue will you - please?'
'Yes, I'll have one, though I think it is most a load of tosh,
But I hope you sell them all before you freeze.'

A MAGICAL FEELING

It had rained and rained for many a day,
As I wandered down the track,
When in the soup of the mire and clay,
I slipped and fell flat on my back.

And I hit my head on a lump of rock,
That stood out of the sea of mud,
And a magical feeling came over me then,
As I lay in the soil and blood.

I was looping the loop in a star-strewn sky,
Where no one had gone before,
When my hands squeezed cold and chilling paste
 - I was back in the mud and gore.

And I heard the sound of the herd of cows
That use that farmyard lane.
With a wrench and a suck I became unstuck
Ignoring discomfort and pain.

Back then I staggered away from that track.
My senses still were reeling.
But I am sure I'll not forget
That moment of magical feeling!

WINNING THE LOTTERY

What shall I do if I win the lottery?
Buy myself some priceless pottery?
A real old master I could buy
And everyone could wonder why
I liked that one at all.

I'd sell my house and buy another.
I'd give this old one to my brother.
I'd have an indoor swimming pool.
Of course, I wouldn't be a fool,
And give it all away.

I'd cruise around the world, I think.
I wouldn't spend it all on drink.
I'd buy a diamond solitaire.
I'd eat too much. I wouldn't care
What anybody said.

Of fashion clothes I'd buy the best.
I must look smarter than the rest.
I'd take my best friends out to dine
And they will tell me I look fine.
But what of you?

What shall I do if I win the lottery?
I'd give new eyes to Mr Ottery.
I'd build a new church hall that's light,
And rooms above both large and bright
If I was rich.

Poor women having many babies
And all the poor with AIDS and scabies,
Children abused and animals beaten,
Everyone who hasn't eaten
I'd give to help.

People who live in cardboard boxes,
Animals chased and killed like foxes,
The old and those who feel the cold,
Those who die where drugs are sold.
But Methodists don't gamble.

MISSING THE MARK

I shouted, screamed and stamped my feet.
I would not hear, although I knew
The voice that told me I'd done wrong
Was true.

She waited till I had calmed down.
She dried my tears and took my hand.
She knew I'd tried to shut her out.
She'd understand.

The years went by; another love
My selfishness had caused to grieve.
I would not listen while she said,
'I'll leave.'

And yet another Love stands by
Throughout my life, but I won't hear.
I'll fill my life with jarring noise,
From fear.

From morn till night I'll hear this noise,
Lest what He's saying takes me o'er,
And I am sold to love, and mine,
No more.

This voice of Love is only heard
In the quiet silence of the soul.
When will I start to listen? Be
Made whole?

MARY - MOTHER TO BE

There's less than a week to go,
And the burden is heavy and great.
Will the coming of God's son cause me pain?
And will He come early or late?
Will He truly be a king?
And what will that mean for me?
For I cannot imagine myself in a court
Of a palace and, down on their knee,
The great and the Lords of the land
Giving homage to my little one,
And those who had thought they were first
Will find they are last - there are none
Who quite know how I feel as I wait,
As the kick of his feet make me gasp.
There's a feeling of joy, and foreboding of sorrow
As I wish His small fingers to clasp.
For God's way is not ours to see.
It's exciting to know that He's there.
He'll be holding my hand when I bring forth His son.
Will you follow Him too? Will you dare?

MARY JOAN

The years were hard on Mary Joan,
The Lord had His hand on her life.
There was little time for sitting back.
There was lots of struggle and strife.

She had handed her life over to the Lord,
And He had tried to explain
That to be as He wanted her to be
Would involve much sorrow and pain.

And because she wanted to be like Him,
She had borne all His discipline well.
She looked forward to being with Christ in Heaven
More than ever she liked to tell.

For Mary Joan was a lonely soul,
Who'd lived by herself for years,
And few there were who gave her a thought,
Or shared her joys or tears.

They left her out of their list of guests.
They left her out of their talk.
They didn't value what she had to say,
Nor called when they went for a walk.

But Mary Joan, she loved her Lord,
And the day it came to be
When she found she had left this life behind.
Before her now what did she see?

A fantastic crowd of people stood
And sang and then bowed down
To the One Who sat upon a throne,
To the One with the beautiful crown.

And Mary Joan sang along with them
And laughed with a great delight,
For what was this she felt on her head
That fitted her head just right?

She reached up her hand and lifted it off
 - A crown of a wondrous hue,
Her crown! The crown that her life had gained,
But Mary Joan just knew

That the crown that sparkled in her hands
Was worn through the Love of the Lord
And she laid it down at the feet of Him,
Who she worshipped and adored.

JARIUS' DAUGHTER

O, husband dear, our child is ill,
I think she's going to die.
Her breathing worsens every hour,
I think her death is nigh.

Dear wife, we must not give up hope,
You really must not cry.
For twelve short years we've cherished her;
We cannot let her die.

There is a man called Jesus, dear.
He'll cure her in a wink.
I'll send my servant out at once
To ask Him here, I think.

The servant went as he was bid,
Found Jesus teaching there.
'Come quickly to my masters' house,
To heal his daughter fair.'

So Jesus went, but on the way
A lady, sick for years,
Touched the corner of His robe,
Despite her many fears.

Then Jesus stopped, 'Who touched Me now?'
The woman had to own
That is was she who sought His help.
He healed her, He alone.

'Too late, too late,' a servant said,
'The little girl is dead.'
'She's only sleeping,' Jesus said.
Cried they, 'You're off Your head.'

He put them out, and taking only
Peter, James and John
He went to where the maiden lay.
Lord, how His halo shone.

He took her gently by the hand
And she sat up in bed.
'Now give her something nice to eat;
She's risen from the dead!'

MEMORIES

The smell of fresh bread, as it wafts up the street.
Can you remember?
The smell of fresh coffee, just ground in the shop.
Can you recall?
The smell of fresh hay as you walk in the meadow.
Brought to memory at all?

The smell of each Christmas, of cooking and spices,
Of candles and cakes,
The magic of panto, the smell of the greasepaint,
Do we enjoy?
The smell of the sea, and the sweetness of heather,
No years can destroy.

MOSES

The sun was hot and there was little shade,
Just a few thorn bushes shimmering in the heat.
When suddenly a fire sprang up from one,
And up jumped Moses from his rocky seat.

He'd seen these fires before when heat was fierce,
And all too soon the bush was burnt and dead.
But, flame enfolded yet this bush remained.
Moses went closer - how was the fire fed?

'Stay Moses,' came the voice within the fire,
'Take off your shoes, for where you are I AM,
For this is Holy ground, and what you see
I AM, your God - you are My chosen man.'

God then showed Moses what his job would be,
And Moses paled in knowledge of that work,
He wriggled like a fish upon a hook,
But in the end his call he did not shirk.

Ah, yes, what of the bush you ask.
Did it survive the heavenly fire and flame?
Why, yes it did and tender shoots put forth.
But Moses, he could never be the same.

Goshen he left with Aaron too beside,
And sought his people who were sore oppressed,
And led them out towards the promised land,
Till God, who called him, took him to his rest.

NEWS

The Christmas cards are here again
With scenes of jolly days,
Of snow and robins, Santa Claus,
And sheep on frozen ways.

Oh, here's a card from Uncle Tom.
He's just returned from Chad.
He flew there after seeing Mike,
Who's gone to Hyderabad.

While Sue is teaching English to
The poor in Lithuania,
Robert's taking expertise to firms
In cold Romania.

Say, look at this, Lord what a card,
It's been through storm and rain.
Sri Lanka - can you read the stamp?
To hell and back again.

It's John, he's fine, he's coming home,
He thinks, though he's not sure.
The first we'll know, he'll just turn up,
And breeze in through the door.

Ah - Matty's died - I'm not surprised.
She wasn't well last year.
At last she's out of Charlie's hair,
And has no more to fear.

Fan and Tim have been to Greece,
They found it far too hot.
They much preferred Sardinia.
They want to buy a yacht.

So on and on then through the pile.
I read of what they've done,
Of where they've been, and how they went
To potter in the sun.

But what of Christmas in all this?
God's Son, who has been born
To save us all from sin and death
All on a Christmas morn?

Do they and we send cards to say
Rejoice for God is here?
Or just 'See me, I and myself.
Where shall we go next year?'

PASSOVER

Do you remember the smell of the donkey?
Do you remember the smell?
Do you remember the shout of the children
As they ran pell-mell
Down to the crowd that was mobbing the Master,
Down to take palms from the trees,
Waving them slowly, then waving them faster,
Laughing and joyful,
At ease?

Do you remember the smell of the Temple?
Do you remember the smell?
Do you remember His eyes and His anger,
Worse than I ever could tell?
Whipping the merchants and spilling the coins
Driving them out of the place,
Showing His strength as He girt up His loins,
Master of Time and of Space?

Do you remember the smell of the olives?
Do you remember the smell?
Do you remember the peace of the evening?
Do you remember it well?
Pools of the moonlight upon the stones falling.
Him on His knees in the grass,
Pallid and weary, while on the Lord calling
That this dread hour may pass.

Do you remember the smell of the blood?
Do you remember the smell?
Do you remember that those who are hung,
Cursed are and finish in hell?
Do you remember the flies and the dust?
Do you remember the gloom?
Making us feel that this was the last
Day - and the future - the tomb.

Can you forget the smell of the flowers?
Can you forget the smell?
Can you forget the song of the birds,
And the sound of the morning bell?
As we, astonished by words that we heard,
Ran to each other to say
'Jesus is Risen' - that is the word
Passed round the city today.

THE POOL OF BETHESDA

Day began as any other
Lying on that rotten bed.
Constant aching in my body,
Constant pain in neck and head.

Lying underneath those arches
By the pool, around me, stone,
Forty years I had been crippled,
Starved of friendship, all alone.

Now and then an angel coming,
Stirred the waters with his hand.
First in after would find healing.
O, if only I could stand.

I had no one who would help me
Get into the pool, like this
Slowly, slowly I would wriggle,
Hope to win a state of bliss.

But another beat me to it
Time and time and time again,
Till I wearied of the effort
To escape this life of pain.

Then He stood there right beside me,
And looked down into my face,
With those eyes so full of pity,
Full of beauty, full of grace.

Do you want to be made better?
Do you want to be made well?
Do I? What a silly question.
'Would you like to live in hell?'

But I told Him of my trouble,
And how I was always last,
And those eyes reflected to me
All my sinnings of the past.

But I knew then that this stranger
Loved me more than I could say,
And He healed me in that moment.
Then He turned and walked away.

Others wait beside the water.
They did not His glance receive.
Judgement I received - with mercy.
Love that leads me to believe.

OUR RAILWAY

If you have some days to spare,
Travel on our railway,
Slowly going anywhere,
Or not.

Here the trains are old and sick.
Travel on our railway.
Stop, or slow, and never quick,
The lot.

Take some food, none's on the train.
Travel on our railway.
Pick the daisies, watch the rain;
Each spot.

Change, when one train pops its clogs.
Travel on our railway.
Country's going to the dogs,
With grot.

Travel any other way, but
Travel on our railway.
Takes you longer still, they say,
By yacht.

THE SEAGULL

I was brought up in a battlefield
Of feathers, beaks and claws,
That murder those who threaten them,
For here there are no laws.

Screaming with hunger and needing food,
I follow my mother's flight,
As she turns and dives in the freshening wind,
Like a flash of grey and white.

And I test my wings to rival hers,
That are shaped to cut through the air,
With grace and a speed that thrills us through.
Such joy you cannot share.

Oh, we're disliked by the world of men
Who hate our noise and greed.
Though our shape inspired a fighting plane,
Saving men in their hour of need.

Look at my wings as I rise and dip.
I'm part of God's lovely creation.
Be glad of our presence along the shore,
For we helped to save a nation.

THE SEAT 1994

It was placed in the square when the summer was there
And the sky it was blue overhead.
And the children and mothers and plenty of others
Would sit there, so it has been said.

The old and the weary, the bright and the dreary
Would pass gossip on all the day,
While close to the seat and all round their feet
The pigeons would get in the way.

But the bright days have passed, and destruction came fast,
Round the woman who sits on the seat,
With all she possesses the battle harasses
With only a shell at her feet.

And her mind it has fled clean out of her head,
And she sits disregarding the storm.
She has nowhere to go and no one to know,
A desolate form on a form.

EARLY SPRING - SCILLY

A thrush sings loudly,
Staking his claim upon the sumach tree,
While mournfully the fog horn blows its single note,
Over the sea the sea-gulls wail and cry,
And here a wren sings fit to burst his throat.

What matter he thinks
Since now the day is not so windy cold,
If drizzle still descends out of a murky sky
It's time I staked my territory here.
This is my home. All comers I defy.

SUMMER '95

The fields are white beneath the burning sun,
While trees and hedgerows wilt and flowers die,
But those on holiday still think it fun.
They play and swim where sea-gulls swoop and cry.

For rarely do we have a summer so
Hot and without the usual rain and cold,
When we can venture, unprepared for snow,
Or hurricane, no coats have we to hold.

No rain is near, so we unburdened are.
No macs, nor boots, the minimum we wear.
But use your shades and cream yourselves to bar
The rays that burn. We've got to all take care.

Now hosepipe bans and standpipes, do we hear
Are being used in force in many a place.
For them the Islands do not shed a tear.
They'd suffered long - their water a disgrace.

Short were supplies for them year after year.
But now they need not care how much they use.
They take it from the sea that is so near,
And smile at talk of drought and all that news.

ENGLISH SUMMER

Summer came last week,
The sky, it was blue,
We opened the curtains,
And the sun poured through.

Summer came last week,
The weather grew hot,
We didn't want clothing
So we took off the lot.

Summer came last week.
The ground was hard.
We watered the garden,
And the tubs in the yard.

Summer came last week.
Those who could all left town.
They drove to the beach
To get pink, red and brown.

Summer came last week.
It left yesterday.
It was good while it lasted.
Today it is grey.

SUMMER NIGHT

The night was still.
Tossing and turning in the summer heat
We tried to sleep.
Some slept, their limbs thrown wide, naked from head to feet,
Seeking relief.

There was the will
To lose ourselves in sweet unknowing
And thus to dream,
Until the day awoke us joyful, rosy-hued, with cocks a-crowing.
Welcoming dawn.

We tossed until
The sea-gulls screeching as they woke to feed,
Swooped low outside.
So sweaty hot, and unrefreshed, without the sleep we need,
We rose.

NEW TEETH

Some of my teeth are like the stars,
Yes, they come out at night.
The others are filled with, no, not gold,
But just with metal bright.

For many years they served me well,
Until there came a day
when I discovered half my meals
were being tucked away

Under the plates for further snacks.
I wished to eat alone,
So I could take and wash them free,
And none would hear me moan.

New plates I'd like, yet none would hear.
It wasn't till I'd swallowed
A metal hook from off one plate.
The other quickly followed.

And after months of waiting round
Some new ones now I try.
They drive me nuts. They do not fit,
And what's the reason why?

So back I go time and again,
To get them fitting right.
To wear them now is tolerable.
Discomfort only slight -

Until I eat, when pain takes o'er.
Discomfort only slight?
I'll sell my teeth to anyone,
So long's the price is right!

TEMPTATION

The years had passed. The time had come.
The call to Him was 'Now!'
Now will I glorify my Son,
And He will Me allow
To do My will in Him, and through
The working of that will
I'll save mankind from sin and death,
And He will show you how.

The Son left home and wandered out
Into a lonely place
To think and ponder how He'd work
To bring about that grace.
Could tackle it in several ways,
For instance, He'd give bread
To all the hungry and the poor.
Then all would seek His face.

Aha - Now wait - the Scriptures say
That that is not enough.
The Word of God is needed too
The path to good is rough.
Though hunger gnawed and it was cold
The Son did not give in.
'I will not build success on that
And all that crafty stuff.'

Suppose I did a magic act
Like jumping from a height.
I'd show I couldn't come to harm.
I'd get up quite alright.
Then everyone would worship me
And they would all be saved,
Because I'd tell them what to do.
I'd bring them to the light.

Aha - But they would worship Me
Through fear and not through love.
It isn't what is wanted
By the Holy One above.
You must not think I'd entertain
This very daft idea.
O tempt me not, you wicked one,
And gave the thought a shove.

The Son could see the nations spread
below Him for the taking.
He pondered on those kingdoms there,
Just as the dawn was breaking.
Yes, if He went the Devil's way
Then they could all be His.
His mind made up, He then could eat,
And His thirst could be slaking.

So tired He was, the thought came through
It's easy to give in,
But God alone's my Master,
And He alone will win.
Get out, go now, you Devil.
You have no place with Me.
Yes, it may mean my dying,
But I'll have no truck with sin.

Are we watching for the Devil,
Who ever speaks us fair?
Who is tempting us to evil
When we think he isn't there?
When we think we're doing God's work,
But we're listening to ourselves,
And pride tries hard to win us
I must warn you, then 'Beware.'

THE MIRACLE

They went to hear the Master speak
Out in the desert bare,
And mums and dads and boys and girls,
The world seemed to be there.

They sat in groups upon the ground,
The crowd was bright and jolly.
He showed in stories short and long
The answers to man's folly.

The hours went by and still they stayed.
His stories were so real.
But evening came, the air grew cool -
Now, what about a meal?

'What shall we do?' His friends began,
'If we send them away
They'll faint before they reach the town,
After so long a day.'

The Master said, 'You give them food.'
'Who us? There are so many.'
They looked for food among themselves.
They knew they hadn't any.

Up came a lad of eight or so.
'You can have mine,' he said.
'There's only two small fish, it's true,
Together with some bread.'

The Master took the bread and asked
A blessing on it there.
Likewise the fish the boy had brought.
Then they began to share.

And on and on they gave it out
To all those hungry folk
Who sat upon the grass and ate.
Then Jesus stood and spoke.

'Collect what's left,' He told His friends,
'When they have had enough.'
Twelve baskets they filled up with fish,
And rolls of bread and stuff.

'Wow,' said the boy, 'Wow,' said the crowd,
'That dinner was quite small,
So how did it spread round this lot
And go to feed us all?'

The gifts we have may not be big,
But if we share them round,
A miracle can still take place,
And help for all is found.

THE TOURIST TRADE

Fresh sheets, fresh towels and hoover round,
Fresh tea-bags, coffee, cream.
Then fasten on our smile again.
We work as in a dream.

For those have gone and these will come,
With all their cares and worry.
So hurry, hurry, quickly now,
They must not see our flurry.

When they arrive we coolly smile
And welcome them inside,
And show them to their en-suite rooms,
With cheerfulness and pride.

And on and on, in sun and heat,
With stripping, washing, cooking,
We long to drop and go to sleep,
When nobody is looking.

And those who come right at the end,
Witness our strain and tension.
Then we move as automata,
Our thinking in suspension.

So, if you can, come early on,
June's better than September,
If you want jollity and fun.
It's quieter in December!

HOTEL BREAKFAST

A full English breakfast the brochure had said.
But how should they know, they were French.
The hotel was busy, yes, I give you that,
And the tables were served by one wench.

There was one cup of coffee, which she did pour out,
Then she rushed off to serve a new table.
But ask for another and you could wait on.
To fetch one yourself you weren't able.

A full English breakfast was bacon and egg,
Or cereal, you weren't allowed both,
Unless you paid extra -£2.50 it said.
It certainly left room for growth.

But down in Penzance it was different by far,
For the Cornish know how to give pleasure.
For a quarter the price there was everything right,
And such kindness there was, beyond measure.

A MOTHER

She was a gentle lady, who lived a gentle life.
A loving, caring mother, a faithful, happy wife.

She's cared for others' children before she met her man.
She was a loving mother. She was a super gran.

She had a sense of humour and understood our fun.
She joined in every interest that grew beneath the sun.

She laughed in all our pleasures, and wept when we were sad.
And everything in nature was seen to make her glad.

And everybody liked her. We shall miss her gentle face.
Let us be a little like her, and spread joy in every place.

THE LORD'S PRAYER

Hello, dear Father, our Daddy, our Dad.
All around You's perfection, and near You we're glad.
We remember when tiny, how awesome Dad seemed,
How fearsome his anger, our delight when he beamed,
And we still have some feeling how tiny we are,
Compared to the Maker of sun and of star.

We look round this planet and weep for its sin,
And ask that You'll rule it. Bring Your kingdom in.
And we ask Your perfection may rule in this world,
May be in all hearts, where now evil is curled.
And give us, dear Father, such food as we need,
And all get sufficient - no hunger, no greed.

The sins we've committed we ask You forgive,
As we forgive those who hurt us as we live.
And please do not test us beyond our resisting,
But save us from evil wherever existing.

We give You the honour, the glory, the power,
For always and always, not just for this hour.
Keep near me, dear Father, our Daddy, our Dad,
For round You's perfection, and near You we're glad.